Creative Lives

BEETHOVEN

Joy Roberts

CREATED BY Humans

Published in 2026 by The Rosen Publishing Group, Inc.
2544 Clinton Street, Buffalo, NY 14224

Portions of this work were originally authored by Joan Stoltman and published as *Beethoven.* All new material in this edition is authored by Joy Roberts.

Editor: Greg Roza
Designer: Michael Flynn

Photo Credits: Cover https://commons.wikimedia.org/wiki/File:Ludwig_Van_Beethoven_LCCN2003663902.jpg; (series background) Yuliya Chsherbakova/Shutterstock.com; p. 5 The Picture Art Collection/Alamy; p. 7 Bennian/Shutterstock.com; p. 9 https://commons.wikimedia.org/wiki/File:Ludwig_van_Beethoven,_aged_twenty-six_(1796).jpg; p. 11 https://commons.wikimedia.org/wiki/File:Leopold_Radoux,_Lodewijk_van_Beethoven,_1773.jpg; p. 13 Diego Grandi/Shutterstock.com; p. 15 Karasev Viktor/Shutterstock.com; p. 17 https://commons.wikimedia.org/wiki/File:Beethovenhome.JPG; p. 19 https://commons.wikimedia.org/wiki/File:Beethoven.jpg; p. 21 PhotoFires/Shutterstock.com.

Cataloging-in-Publication Data
Names: Roberts, Joy, 1978-.
Title: Beethoven / Joy Roberts.
Description: Buffalo, NY : Created by Humans, an imprint of Rosen Publishing, 2026. | Series: Creative lives | Includes glossary and index.
Identifiers: ISBN 9781534552395 (pbk.) | ISBN 9781534552401 (library bound) | ISBN 9781534552418 (ebook)
Subjects: LCSH: Beethoven, Ludwig van, 1770-1827--Juvenile literature. | Composers--Austria--Biography--Juvenile literature.
Classification: LCC ML3930.B4 R63 2026 | DDC 780.92--dc23

Manufactured in the United States of America

CPSIA Compliance Information: Batch #CWCBH26. For Further Information contact Rosen Publishing at 1-800-237-9932.

CONTENTS

Music in His Heart

Music great Ludwig van Beethoven once said: "What I have in my heart must come out; that is the reason why I **compose**." Beethoven lived hundreds of years ago, but he is still honored today for his creative life!

Early Life

Beethoven was born on December 16, 1770. He lived with his family in the city of Bonn, which is part of what's now the country of Germany. Beethoven was named after his grandfather who was a **famous** musician.

Odense
Groningen
Hamburg
NETH.
Bremen
Elbe
Nijmegen
Hannover
Oder
Düsseldorf
BERLIN
GERMANY
Bonn
Leipzig
Dresden
Frankfurt am Main
PRAGUE
Nuremberg
Stuttgart
CZECH REPUBLIC
Munich
Salzburg
Danube
Alps
Innsbruck

Beethoven's father wanted his son to be a musician too. Beethoven had to practice for hours each day. He learned many **instruments** and became talented at playing the piano. By age seven, Beethoven was playing in front of people.

Beethoven's grandfather died when Beethoven was young. The family began to have trouble with money. Beethoven left school around age 11, but he kept studying music. He learned from the court **organ** player in Bonn. Beethoven also began composing music.

Beethoven's grandfather,

Ludwig van Beethoven

Visiting Vienna

Beethoven had already written a **complete** piece of music by the time he was 12. In 1787, he was sent to Vienna, Austria, the center of the music world. He was supposed to study with the famous composer Mozart. Then, Beethoven's mother fell ill. Beethoven went back home.

Beethoven's birthplace

Beethoven continued to play music. He started teaching music too. He met many important people through his music. In 1792, Beethoven returned to Vienna, where he soon became known as a great piano player.

A Composer

While in Vienna, Beethoven took time to learn from other musicians. He began to work more on composing music. Beethoven soon became more famous for his composing than he was for playing the piano. His **career** was off to a good start.

A Great Loss

Around age 25, Beethoven began to go deaf, or lose his hearing. He didn't think he could live without hearing. But he knew he still had a lot of music left to write. In fact, he went on to compose some of his greatest works after he had already gone deaf.

Honored Artist

Before Beethoven, many composers thought **melodies** were for singing. But Beethoven wrote melodies for instruments. His music was also very emotional, or full of feelings. His work played a big part in making music a true art form!

GLOSSARY

career: The job someone chooses to do for a long time.

complete: Having all the parts.

compose: To write music.

famous: Well-known.

instrument: An object used to make music.

melody: A pleasing series of musical notes that form the main part of a song or piece of music.

organ: A musical instrument that has a keyboard and pipes of different lengths and makes sound by pushing air through the pipes.

FOR MORE INFORMATION

BOOKS

Mallett, Richard. *Children's Book of Music*. New York, NY: DK Publishing, 2023.

Mattern, Joanne. *Ludwig van Beethoven*. Egremont, MA: Red Chair Press, 2025.

WEBSITES

Ludwig van Beethoven
www.kennedy-center.org/education/resources-for-educators/classroom-resources/media-and-interactives/artists/beethoven-ludwig-van/
Read even more details about the life of Beethoven.

Museum
www.beethoven.de/en/museum
You can visit a museum all about Beethoven in Bonn, Germany, to learn more.

INDEX